HAMLET:

PRINCE OF PIGS

WITH WORDS BY

WILLIAM SHAKESPEARE

AND

WITH SUBTRACTIONS & DRAWINGS
BY SARAH BOYER

Bunncoco Press

How Hamlet Became My Prince of Pigs

Another *Hamlet*? There must be a million *Hamlet*s already. Slang *Hamlet*. Illustrated *Hamlet*. First folio *Hamlet*. Compressed *Hamlet*. No Fear *Hamlet*. Into this crowded field, I toss *Hamlet Prince of Pigs: A Tragic Comic Strip*.

Why a comic strip? Plays and comics are uncannily alike, two arts seemingly separated at birth. Both use visual expression and words to get across their meaning. Both like to refer to their own medium – plays to plays and comics to comics. (Think of the play within the play.) Both have abrupt breaks between scenes. And in both the words are almost all dialogue, with practically no narration. These two arts are made for each other!

But why turn Hamlet into a pig? First because of the pun. In the name "Hamlet" I hear Ham-let, little ham, little pig. And the pig pun fits! In Shakespeare's day, the usual mask for a king, if you wanted to make fun of him, was a pig mask. In *Will in the World: How Shakespeare Became Shakespeare,* Stephen Greenblatt notes that in sixteenth-century England, the "swine-snouted king" was a stock theater figure and that Nick Bottom's ass mask in *Midsummer Night's Dream,* "strikingly recalls the swine's snout placed on the face of the king."

So, you see, Hamlet simply had to be a pig. And once that was set, all the other animals fell into place. I followed a one-family, one-species rule. Thus Hamlet's uncle, Claudius, the one who killed Hamlet's father, would be a big fat hog, or as Shakespeare put it, "the bloat king." His mother, Gertrude, who married her husband's murderer, would also be a pig, but a pig with lipstick. For Ophelia's family, I figured that since she dies in water, she should be some kind of cat, and so should her father, Polonius, and her brother, Laertes. Rosencrantz and Guildenstern would be weasels because they are, you know, weaselly.

I also decided that each profession would be represented by one species. Thus the gravediggers would be dogs because dogs are excellent diggers. The actors would be mice because they act in a play called "The Mousetrap." The guards would be rats because, well, rats look nice in helmets.

You will notice that although I have taken the liberty of turning all the humans into animals, I have not changed the language. All the words here are Shakespeare's. There are no substitutions or additions. Why? Because if you try to make Shakespeare easier by translating the words into easier words, it's no longer Shakespeare. It's some kind of mush with bits of Shakespeare's plot and language floating around in it, and that's distasteful.

Thus, I made myself a motto in simplifying Shakespeare's text: Only subtract. Or to put it in Queen Gertrude's words (when she speaks to Polonius): More art with less matter! The big question, of course, was what to leave out and what to leave in. Along with all the major plot points, I kept the big speeches, the famous lines, and, of course, the animal references! "The cat will mew and dog will have his day." Animals always lighten things up.

By the way, a strange thing happens, when you subtract words from *Hamlet;* the tragedy begins to border on comedy. I kid you not. A pared-down *Hamlet* is really a very funny play. Which raises yet another question: Should we be laughing at death, revenge, and mourning? Shakespeare thought it was okay – or at least inevitable. As Greenblatt notes, he learned from the morality plays of his day, "that the boundary between comedy and tragedy is surprisingly porous." (p. 34) So too is the boundary between plays and comic strips, and between Shakespeare's language and our own. Shakespeare gave us a language to play with. So let the play begin!

– *Sarah Boxer*
Washington, D.C., 2019

THE NIGHT WATCH

Who's there?
Not a mouse stirring.
Welcome, Horatio. Welcome, good Marcellus.
What, has this thing appeared again tonight?
I have seen nothing.
Horatio says 'tis but our fantasy.
Tush, tush, 'twill not appear.

... Look where it comes again.
... like the king that's dead.
...speak to it, Horatio.
Looks it not like the king?
Question it, Horatio.

But soft,
behold–lo
where
it comes
again!
Shall I
strike at it
with
my
partisan?
Speak to
me ... O
speak!
'Tis here.
'Tis here.
PROF
'Tis
Gone.

HAMLET'S THOUGHTS

How is it that the clouds still hang on you?
Not so, my lord, I am too much i'th' sun .
Good Hamlet, cast thy nightly colour off, and let thine eye look like a friend on Denmark.
You must know your father lost a father; that father lost, lost his ...
Why should we ... take it to heart?

O that this too too solid flesh would melt,
Thaw, and resolve itself into a dew...
How weary, stale, flat, and unprofitable
Seem to me all the uses of this world!

Fie on't, ah fie, fie!
'Tis an unweeded garden
that grows to seed ...

That it should come to this —
But two months dead — nay, not
so much, not two —

So excellent a king, that was to this
Hyperion to a satyr,
so loving to my mother.

    ... Must I remember?
Why she would hang on him
As if increase of appetite had grown
By what it fed on ...

and yet within a month ... married my
father's brother, but no more like my father
than I to Hercules;
within a month... She married...
But break, my heart,
for I must hold my tongue.

My lord, I came to see your father's funeral.

I prithee do not mock me, fellow student .

Indeed,my lord, it followed hard upon.

I think it was to see my mother's wedding.

I saw him once. He was a goodly king.

He was a man. Take him for all in all, I shall not look upon his like again.

My lord, I think I saw him yesternight.

Saw?

Who?

My lord, the King your father
The King my father?
For God's love let me hear! What looked he? Frowningly?
A countenance more in sorrow than in anger.
Pale or red?
Nay, very pale.
And fixed his eyes upon you ?
Most constantly.
His beard was grizzly, no?
It was as I have seen it in his life, a sable silvered.
I'll watch tonight. Perchance 'twill walk again.

Enter the Ghost

The air bites shrewdly, it is very cold.
It is a nipping and an eager air.
What hour now?
I think it lacks of twelve.
No, it is struck.
Look, my Lord, it comes.
Angels and ministers of grace defend us!
Be thou a spirit of health or goblin damned,
Bring with thee airs from heaven or blasts from hell,
Be thy intents wicked or charitable,
thou com'st in such a questionable shape
that I will speak to thee..
King, father, royal Dane.
O answer me!

Something is rotten in
the state of Denmark.

Speak, I'll go no further.

Mark me.

I will.

My hour is
almost come.

Alas, poor ghost!
Speak. I am bound to hear.
So art thou to revenge when thou shalt hear.
What?
I am thy father's spirit,
Doomed for a certain term
to walk the night. ...
If thou didst ever thy dear
father love --
Oh God!
Revenge his foul and most
unusual murder.
Murder?
Murder most foul...
Now Hamlet, hear...
A serpent stung me.
... The serpent
that did sting thy
father's life
Now wears his crown.
O Hamlet, what a
falling off was there!
Mine
uncle?

O horrible, horrible, most horrible!
O villain, villain, smiling, damned villain!
That one may smile and smile and be a villain. At least I'm sure it may be so in Denmark.... So, uncle, there you are.

Lord Hamlet!
Illo, ho, ho, my lord.
Hillo, ho, ho, boy; come, bird, come.
What news, my lord?
O wonderful!
Good, my lord, tell it.
No, you'll reveal it.
My lord, we will not.
Nay, but swear't ... Upon my sword. ... Never to speak of this that you have seen...
Swear by my sword.
Swear.

O day and night, but this is wondrous strange!
There are more things in heaven and earth, Horatio, than are dreamt of in your philosophy.
How strange or odd soe'er I bear myself...
As I perchance hereafter shall think meet to put an antic disposition on ...
... that you at such time seeing me never shall ... note that you know aught of me...
So grace and mercy at your most need, help you, swear.
Swear.

WHAT A
PIECE OF
WORK

How now, Ophelia, what's the matter?
Alas, my lord, I have been so affrighted.
With what, i' th' name of God?
My lord, as I was sewing in my chamber, Lord Hamlet ... his knees knocking each other and with a look so piteous ... as if he had been loosed out of hell ... comes before me.
Mad for thy love?
My lord, I do not know. But truly I do fear it.

I have found the very cause of Hamlet's lunacy.

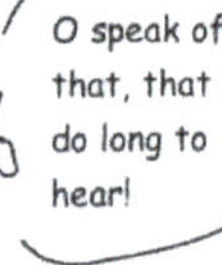

O speak of that, that I do long to hear!

He tells me, my sweet queen, that he hath found the head and source of all your son's distemper.

I doubt it is no other but the main — his father's death and our o'er-hasty marriage.

I will be brief. Your noble son is mad — 'Mad' call I it, for to define true madness, what is't but to be nothing else but mad? ...
    That he is mad, 'tis true; 'tis true 'tis pity, and pity 'tis 'tis true.

But look where sadly the poor wretch comes reading.
How does my good Lord Hamlet? ... Do you know me, my lord?
Excellent, excellent well. You're a fishmonger.
What do you read, my lord?
Words, words, words
What is the matter, my lord?
Between who?
Though this be madness, yet there is method in't ... My lord, I will take my leave of you.
You cannot, sir, take from me anything that I will more willingly part withal — except my life, my life, my life.

I will tell you why. ... I have of late — but wherefore I know not — lost all my mirth. ... This goodly frame, the earth, seems to me a sterile promontory. ...

This most excellent canopy, the air, look you, this brave o'er hanging, this majestical roof fretted with golden fire — why, it appears no other thing to me than a foul and pestilent congregation of vapors.

What a piece of work is a man! How noble in reason, how infinite in faculty, in form and moving how express and admirable, in action how like an angel, in apprehension how like a god — the beauty of the world, the paragon of animals! And yet, to me, what is this quintessence of dust? Man delights not me— no, nor woman neither, though by your smiling you seem to say so.

There are the players...
You're welcome, masters, welcome all. — I am glad to see thee well. ...
We'll hear a play tomorrow.
Can you play the murder of Gonzago?
Ay, my Lord..
We'll ha't tomorrow night. You could for a need study a speech of some ... lines which I would set down and insert in't, could ye not?
Ay, my lord.
My good friends, I'll leave you till night. You are welcome to Elsinore.

Now I am alone.
O, what a rogue
and peasant slave
am I!

Is it not monstrous that this player here,
but in a fiction, in a dream of passion,
could force his soul so ...
tears in his eyes, distraction in his
aspect, a broken voice ...

And all for nothing. For Hecuba! What's
Hecuba to him, or he to Hecuba, that he
should weep for her? What would he do
had he the motive and the cue for passion
that I have? He would drown the stage
with tears...

Yet I, a dull and muddy-mettled rascal ... can say nothing...
Am I a coward?... I am pigeon-livered and lack gall...
Why, what an ass am I?...

I have heard that guilty creatures sitting at a play have by the very
cunning of the scene been struck so to the soul that presently they
have proclaimed their malefactions ...

I'll have these players play something like the murder of my father
before mine uncle . I'll observe his looks .... The play's the thing
wherein I'll catch the conscience of the King.

OPHELIA
IS THE
BAIT

Sweet Gertrude, leave us too, for we have closely sent for Hamlet hither, that he, as 'twere by accident, may here affront Ophelia.
I shall obey you.
And for your part, Ophelia, I do wish that your good beauties be the happy cause of Hamlet's wildness....
Madam, I wish it may.
Ophelia, walk you here... Read on this book...
LA DI DA
I hear him coming. Let's withdraw...

To be or not to be;
that is the question.

Whether 'tis nobler in
the mind to suffer the
slings and arrows of
outrageous fortune, or
to take arms against a
sea of troubles, and by
opposing, end them...

To die, to sleep — No more, and by
a sleep to say we end the heartache
and the thousand natural shocks
that flesh is heir to — 'tis a
consummation devoutly to be wished.

To die, to sleep.
To sleep, perchance to dream.
Ay, there's the rub, for in that
sleep of death what dreams may
come when we have shuffled off
that mortal coil
must give us pause...

But that the dread
of something after death,
the undiscovered country from whose bourn no
traveller returns, puzzles the will,
and makes us rather bear those ills we have than
fly to others that we know not of?

LA DI DA
Soft you, now, the fair Ophelia!
How does your honour for this many a day?
I humbly thank you, well, well, well.
My lord, I have remembrances of yours that I have longed long to redeliver.
No, no . I never gave you aught.
HAMLET'S STUFF
My honored lord, you know right well you did...
Ha ha. Are you honest?
My lord...
Are you fair?
HAMLET'S STUFF

I did love you once.
Indeed, my lord, you made me believe so.
You should not have believed me. ...
I loved you not.
I was the more deceived.
Get thee to a nunnery. ...
Get thee to a nunnery...To a nunnery, go, and quickly, too. ... I say we will have no more marriages. Those that are married already — all but one — shall live. The rest shall keep as they are. To a nunnery, go.
O what a noble mind is here o'erthrown!

31

O woe is me, T'have seen what I have seen, see what I see!
Love? ...
How now, Ophelia?
You need not tell us what Lord hamlet said; we heard it all...
Let his queen mother all alone entreat him to show his griefs. ... and I'll be placed ... in the ear of all their conference.
It shall be so. Madness in great ones should not unwatched go.

HAMLET COACHES THE ACTORS

Speak the speech,
I pray you,
as I pronounced
it to you —
trippingly on
the tongue...
Do not saw the air
too much with your hand...
Be not too tame neither...
Suit the action to the word,
the word to the action...
hold as 'twere the mirror
up to nature...

What ho, Horatio!
Here, sweet lord, at your service.
There is a play tonight before the King. One scene of it comes near the circumstance... of my father's death ...
Observe mine uncle. If his occulted guilt do not unkennel in one speech, it is a damned ghost that we have seen, and my imaginations are as foul as Vulcan's stithy ...

Come hither,
my good Hamlet.
Sit by me.

No, good mother,
here's mettle
more attractive.

Lady, shall I lie in your lap?

I mean my head
upon your lap?

Do you think I
meant country matters?

No, my lord.

Ay, my lord.

I think
nothing, my
lord... You are
merry, my lord.

Who, I?

What should a man do but be
merry? For look you how
cheerfully my mother looks,
and my father died within 's
two hours.

Nay 'tis
twice two
months, my
lord.

So long? ... O heavens, die two
months ago and not forgotten yet?
Then there's hope a great man's
memory might outlive his life half a
year.

I PRESENT
THE PLAY WITHIN THE PLAY
PLEASE DO NOT BE CONFUSED.

YAWN
My spirits grow dull,
and fain I would beguile
the tedious day with sleep.
ZZZ
SHHH
Sleep,
rock
thy
brain.
ZZZZ
SQUIRT
ZZZ
Madam, how like you
this play?
The lady protests too much, methinks.

38

WAKIE WAKIE
NOOOO!
NOOOO!
BOO HOO! OUR KING IS DEAD!
LET'S BE SAD TOGETHER NOW, OK? HUG?
What do you call the play?
The Mousetrap.

This play is the image of a murder done in Vienna.
You are as good as a chorus, my lord.
You shall see anon how the murderer gets the love of Gonzago's wife....
How fares my lord?
What, frighted with false fire?
The king rises.
Give me some light. Away.

THE PLAY
WITHIN THE
PLAY

IS NOW OVER!

O good Horatio, I'll take the Ghost's word for a thousand pound. Didst perceive?
Very well, my lord.
Upon the talk of pois'ning?
I did very well note him.
The Queen your mother, in most great affliction of spirit, hath sent me to you.
My mother, you say? ...
She desires to speak with you in her closet ere you go to bed.

My lord, the Queen would speak with you ...
Do you see yonder cloud that's almost in shape of a camel?
... like a camel, indeed.
Methinks it is like a weasel.
It is backed like a weasel.
Or like a whale.
Very like a whale.

'Tis now the very witching time of night, when churchyards yawn, and   hell itself breathes out contagion
to this world.

Now I could drink hot blood...

Soft now, to my mother...

Let me be cruel, not unnatural.

I will speak daggers to her,

but use none....

POLONIUS
SPIES,
POLONIUS
DIES

My lord, he's going to his mother's closet. Behind the arras I'll convey myself to hear the process.
Thanks, dear my lord.
I'll call upon you ere you go to bed, and tell you what I know .
O, my offence is rank! It smells to heaven...A brother's murder. Pray can I not...
Is there not rain enough in the sweet heavens to wash it white as snow?...

O, what form of prayer can serve my turn?
'Forgive me my foul murder'?
That cannot be, since I am still possessed of those effects for which I did the murder —my crown, mine own ambition, and my queen.
Bow, stubborn knees.... All may be well.
Now I might do it pat, now he is praying, and now I'll do't...
And so he goes to heaven....
My words fly up, my thoughts remain below.
Words without thoughts never to heaven go.

Now, mother, what's the matter?
Hamlet, thou hast thy father much offended.
Mother, you have my father much offended.
Why, how now, Hamlet? ... Have you forgot me?
No ... you are the Queen, your husband's brother's wife.
But — would you were not... you are my mother.
Come, come, and sit you down. You shall not budge.
What wilt thou do?

You go not until I set you up a glass where you may see the inmost part of you.
What wilt thou do? Thou wilt not murder me?
What ho! Help, help, help!
Help, help, ho!
How now, a rat?
Dead for a ducat, dead.
O, I am slain!
Nay, I know not. Is it the King?
O me, what hast thou done?

O, what a rash and bloody deed is this!
A bloody deed — almost as bad, good mother, as kill a king and marry with his brother.
As kill a king?
Ay, lady, 'twas my word.
Thou wretched, rash, intruding fool, farewell.
Leave wringing of your hands. Peace, sit you down, and let me wring your heart.

HAMLET BERATES HIS MOTHER

See what a grace was seated
on this brow —
Hyperion's curls, the front of
Jove himself, an eye like
Mars,
to threaten or
command,
a station
like the herald
Mercury new lighted on a
heaven-kissing hill ...This *was*
your husband.

Look you now what
follows. Here *is* your
husband, like a mildewed ear
blasting his wholesome brother.
     Have you eyes? ...
What judgment would step from
this to this?

O, speak to me no more! These words like daggers enter in mine ears. No more, sweet Hamlet. ...
Save me and hover o'er me with your wings.
DADDY!
Alas, he's mad.
Do not forget. This visitation is but to whet thy almost blunted purpose.
But look, amazement on thy mother sits. O, step between her and her fighting soul. ... Speak to her, Hamlet.

How is it with you, lady?
Alas, how is't with you, that you do bend your eye on vacancy and with th' incorporal air do hold discourse?
Whereon do you look?
Do not look upon me.
On him, on him. Look you how pale he glares.
Do you see nothing there?
Nothing at all, yet all that is I see.
Why, look you there. Look how it steals away. My father ... as he lived. ...

It is not madness that I have uttered. ... Confess yourself to heaven. ...
And do not spread the compost o'er the weeds to make them ranker.
O Hamlet thou hast cleft my heart in twain!
O, throw away the worser part of it,
And live the purer with
the other half!
What shall I do?
Let the bloat King tempt you again to bed... call you his mouse, and let him for a pair of reechy kisses ... make you to ravel all this matter out, that I essentially am not in madness. ... 'Twere good you let him know.

Mad as the sea and wind when both contend which is the
mightier. In his lawless fit, behind the arras hearing something
stir, he whips out his rapier out and cries,'A rat, a rat,' and in
his brainish apprehension kills the unseen good old man.

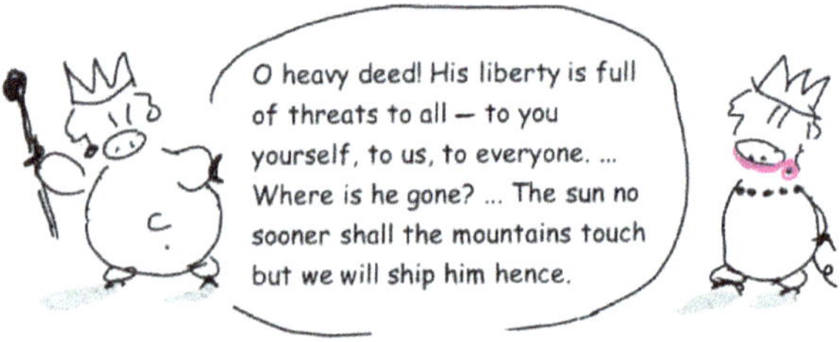

HAMLET BURIES THE BODY

Safely stowed.
What have you done, my lord, with the dead body?
My lord, you must tell us where the body is, and go with us to the King.
The body is with the King, but the King is not with the body.
A thing?
The King is a thing.

Now, Hamlet, where's Polonius?
At supper.
At supper? Where?
Not where he eats, but where he is eaten. ...
... A certain convocation of politic worms are e'en at him ... We fat all creatures else to fat us, and we fat ourselves for maggots. Your fat King and your lean beggar is but variable service -- two dishes but to one table. That's the end.
A man may fish with the worm that hath eat of a king, and eat of the fish that hath fed of that worm.

What dost thou mean by this?

Nothing but to show you how a king may go a progress through the guts of a beggar.

Where is Polonius?
In heaven. ...
If your messenger find him not there, seek him i'th' other place yourself.

But indeed, if you find him not this month, you shall nose him as you go up the stairs into the lobby.
Hamlet, this deed of thine ... must send thee hence ...Therefore prepare thyself. The barque is ready, and the wind at help ... and everything is bent for England.

PYOOO!

For England?

OPHELIA LOSES HER MIND

O, this is the poison of deep grief! It springs all from her father's death. O Gertrude, Gertrude, when sorrows come they come not single spies, but in battalions ...

First, her father slain; next, your son gone, and he most violent author of his own just remove. ... poor Ophelia divided from herself and her fair judgement.

Where is the king? ... O thou vile King, give me my father.
Calmly, good Laertes.
Tell me Laertes, why thou art incensed. -- Let him go, Gertrude. --
Speak, man.
Where is my father?
Dead
But not by him.
I am guiltless of your father's death and am most sensibly in grief for it.
How came he dead? I'll not be juggled with.
How now, what noise is that?

They bore him barefaced
on the bier, hey non nony,
nony hey nony, and in his
grave rained many a tear -
-Fare you well my dove.

You must sing 'Down, a
down', and you, 'Call him
down-a-down-a.,
... There's rosemary,
that's for remembrance.
... And there is pansies;
that's for thoughts.

There's fennel for you, and
columbines. There's rue for you,
and here's some for me ... O you
must wear your rue with a
difference. There's a daisy. I
would give you some violets, but
they withered all when my
father died ... For bonny sweet
Robin is all my joy... And will a
not come again, and will a not
come again? No, no, he is dead.
... He never will come again.

LAERTES SEEKS REVENGE

Do you see this, O God? ... His means of death, his obscure burial -- no trophy, sword, nor hatchment o'er his bones ... that I must call't in question.
WHoSH
So you shall; and where the offence is, let the great axe fall.
You must put me in your heart for friend ... He which hath your noble father slain pursued my life ...
It well appears. But tell me why you proceeded not against these feats...?
O, for two special reasons ... The Queen his mother lives almost by his looks ... The other motive ... is the great love the general gender bear him ... So that my arrows would have reverted to my bow again, and not where I had aimed them.

And so I have a noble father lost, a sister driven into desp'rate terms ... But my revenge will come.
Laertes, was your father dear to you?
Or are you like the painting of a sorrow, a face without a heart?
Why ask you this?
Hamlet comes back. What would you undertake to show yourself your father's son in deed more than in words?
To cut his throat i'th' church.

Good Laertes, will you do this? --
Keep close within your chamber.
Hamlet returned shall
know you are come home ...

I will do't,
and for
that
purpose
I'll anoint
my sword.

He ... most generous, and free
from all contriving, will not peruse the
foils; so that with ease, or with a little
shuffling, you may choose a sword
unbated, and in a pass of practice,
requite him for your father.

... I'll touch my point
with this contagion ...
if I gall him slightly,
it may be death.

There is a willow grows aslant a brook ... Therewith fantastic garlands did she make of cross-flowers, nettles, daisies, and long purples ... There on the pendant boughs her crownet weeds clamb'ring to hang, an envious sliver broke, when down the weedy trophies and herself fell in the weeping brook.

Her clothes spread wide, and mermaid-like a while they bore her up; which time she chanted snatches of old tunes... till that her garments, heavy win their drink, pulled the poor wretch from her melodious lay to muddy death.

IN THE GRAVEYARD

Here lies the water -- good. Here stands the man -- good. If the man go to this water and drown himself, it is, will he nill he, he goes. Mark you that. But if the water come to him and drown him, he drowns not himself; argal he that is not guilty of his own death shortens not his own life.

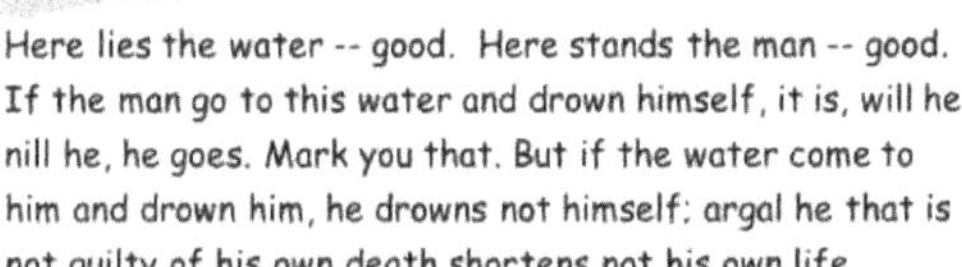

That skull had a tongue in it and could sing once. How the Knave jowls it to th' ground...!
X+
DIG DIG
What man dost thou dig it for?
For no man, sir.
What woman, then?
For none, neither.
Who is to be buried in't?
How absolute the knave is! We must speak by the card, or equivocation will undo us...
One that was a woman, sir; but rest her soul she's dead.

How long hast thou been a grave — maker?
How long is that since?
I came to't that day that our last King Hamlet o'ercame Fortinbras.
Cannot you tell that? Every fool can tell that. It was the very day that young Hamlet was born — he that was mad and sent to England.
Ay, marry, why was he sent to England?
Why, because a was mad. A shall recover his wits there; or if a do not, 'tis no great matter there.
How came he mad?
Very strangely, They say .
WAG WAG
How strangely?... Upon what ground?
Why, here in Denmark.

How long will a man lie i'th'earth ere he rot?
I'faith if a be not rotten before a die ... a will last you some eight year or nine year.
Here's a skull, now. This skull has lain in the earth three and twenty years.
Whose was it?
Whose do you think it was?
Nay, I know not
This same skull, sir, was Yorick's skull, the King's jester.
This?
E'en that.
Let me see.

Alas, poor Yorick, I knew him, Horatio -- a fellow of infinite jest, of most excellent fancy. He hath borne me on his back a thousand times...

Here hung those lips that I have kissed I know not how oft.

Where be your gibes now, your gambols, your songs, your flashes of merriment that were wont to set the table on a roar?

To what base uses we may return, Horatio! Why may not imagination trace the noble dust of Alexander till a find it stopping a bung hole? ... Imperial Caesar, dead and turned to clay, might stop a hole to keep the wind away.

SWEETS
TO THE
SWEET

Here comes the King, the Queen, the courtiers -- Who is that they follow, and with such maimed rites?
Couch we a while, and mark ... ...That is Laertes, a very noble youth, mark.
Must there be no more done?
No more be done.
Lay her i'the earth. And from her fair and unpolluted flesh may violets spring.
I tell thee, churlish priest, A minist-ring angel shall my sister be, when thou lie howling.
What, the fair Ophelia?

Sweets to the sweet. Farewell. I hoped thou shouldst have been my Hamlet's wife ...
I thought thy bride-bed to have decked, sweet maid, and not t'have strewed thy grave.
O treble woe fall ten times treble on that cursed head whose wicked deed thy most ingenious sense deprived thee of!

Hold off the earth a while till I have caught her in my arms once more ...
Now pile up your dust upon the quick and dead.
What is he whose grief ... conjures the wand'ring stars?
This is I, Hamlet the Dane.

The devil take thy soul.
Thou prayest not well. I prithee take thy fingers from my throat...
Pluck them asunder.
I loved Ophelia. Forty thousand brothers could not, with all their quantity of love, make up my sum. -- What wilt thou do for her ?
O, he is mad, Laertes
Woot weep, woot fight, woot fast, woot tear thyself, woot drink up eisel, eat a crocodile?...
Let Hercules himself do what he may, the cat will mew and dog will have his day.

HAMLET AGREES TO A DUEL

I am very sorry, good Horatio, that to Laertes I forgot myself; but sure, the bravery of his grief did put me in tow'ring passion.
SCOOTCH SCOOTCH
Your lordship is right welcome back to Denmark.
I humbly thank you, sir.
I should impart a thing to you from his majesty.
I will receive it, sir, with all diligence of spirit. Put your bonnet to his right use; 'tis for the head.
I thank your lordship, 'tis very hot.
No believe me, 'tis very cold.
It is indifferent cold, my lord, indeed.
Methinks it is very sultry and hot for my complexion.

My Lord, his majesty bade me signify to you that a has laid a great wager on your head. ...
You are not ignorant of what excellence Laertes is at his weapon.
What's his weapon?
Rapier and dagger.
That's two of his weapons. But well....
Let the foils be brought.
You will lose this wager, my lord.
I do not think so. ... I have been in continual practice, I shall win at the odds.
There's a special providence in the fall of a sparrow.
If it be now, 'tis not to come. If it be not to come, it will be now. If it be not now, yet it will come. The readiness is all.

LOOKS LIKE AN ANGRY MOB....
Give me your pardon, sir. I've done you wrong...
Was't Hamlet wronged Laertes? Never Hamlet. ... Who does it then? His madness.
I do receive your offered love like love and will not wrong it.
SQUEAK!
I do freely embrace it.

Give us the foils. Come on.
Come, one for me.
I'll be your foil, Laertes. ...
You mock me, sir.
ENVENOMED FOIL TO POISON HAMLET
This is too heavy; let me see another..
This likes me well. ...

DRINKING THE KOOL-AID

Set me the stoups of wine upon that table.
OOH WINE!
AND KOOL-AID!
Now the King drinks to Hamlet.

GLUG GLUG
GEE I COULD USE A DRINK TOO...
Come on, sir.
One.
Another hit. What say you?
Come, my lord.
No.
A touch a touch, I do confess.
A hit, a very palpable hit.
Our son shall win.
The Queen carouses to thy fortune, Hamlet.
Good madam.

Gertrude, do not drink.
I will, my lord, I pray you pardon me.
It is the poisoned cup; it is too late.
GLUG GLUG
WHAT DID YOU SAY, DEAR?
WANNA SIP, HAMLET?
I dare not drink yet, madam; by and by.
Come, let me wipe thy face.

THE
DUEL

My Lord, I'll hit him now.
I do not think't.
And yet 'tis almost 'gainst my conscience,
Come for the third, Laertes, you but dally.
Say you so? Come on. ... Have at you now!

POISONED SWORD MEANT TO KILL HAMLET
TO KILL OR NOT TO KILL?
Part them...
CLANG
ZING
SHWING
CLATTER
GOTCHA!
YEOW!
I am justly killed by my own treachery.
POISONED SWORD MEANT TO KILL HAMLET

Look to the
Queen there, ho!

How does the
Queen?

She swoons
to see them
bleed.

No, no, the drink, the
drink! O my dear
Hamlet, the drink, the
drink — I am poisoned.

O villainy! Ho! Let
the door be locked!

SCOOTCH
SCOOTCH

EVERYONE
DIES

Treachery, seek it out.
It is here, Hamlet. Hamlet, thou art slain.
The treacherous instrument is in thy hand, unbated and envenomed. The foul practice hath turned itself on me.
Lo, here I lie, never to rise again.
Thy mother's poisoned. ... The King, the King's to blame.
The point envenomed too?
Then, venom, to thy work.

Here, thou incestuous,
murd'rous Dane,
drink off this potion.

Follow my mother.

Exchange
forgiveness with
me, noble
Hamlet. Mine
and my father's
death come not
upon thee, nor
thine on me.

Heaven make
thee free of it!

I follow thee.
I am dead, Horatio. Had I but time — O, I could tell you — But let it be, Horatio, I am dead, thou liv'st. Report me and my cause aright to the unsatisfied.
Here's yet some liquor left.
As thou'rt a man, give me the cup. Let go ... If thou didst ever hold me in thy heart, absent thee from felicity a while, and in this harsh world draw thy breath in pain to tell my story.

O, I die, Horatio!
The rest is silence.
... O, O, O, O!
Now cracks a
noble heart.
Good night,
sweet
prince.